UNREASONABLE DOUBT

A True Story of Conscience, Conviction, and Grace

UNREASONABLE DOUBT

When the Call of Duty Becomes a Test of Faith

Gregg A. Stewart

THE STEWART HOUSE
Grace. Truth. Light.

Book Design & Production:
Columbus Publishing Lab
www.ColumbusPublishingLab.com

For permission requests, contact:
greggstewart1@gmail.com

Paperback ISBN: 979-8-90183-036-9
Hardcover ISBN: 979-8-90183-061-1
E-book ISBN: 979-8-90183-037-6

Printed in the United States of America
1 3 5 7 9 10 8 6 4 2

DISCLAIMER

This work is a personal memoir. The accounts, dialogue, and descriptions are based on the author's recollections, notes, and impressions from the trial of *State of Ohio v. Muata M. Fisher* and related experiences. While every effort has been made to ensure accuracy, memory is an imperfect witness.

This book is not a verbatim transcript, official court record, or comprehensive legal account. Names, dates, and identifying details have been adapted or omitted in certain cases to preserve privacy and protect individuals' dignity.

The reflections contained herein are offered not as legal commentary or formal theological doctrine, but as one man's testimony to the intersection of faith, justice, and conscience. Nothing herein should be construed as a statement on ongoing legal matters or appeals.

The views expressed are solely those of the author.

DEDICATION

To my wife, Stephanie—whose steadfast faith and quiet strength are the pillars beneath every page.

To my daughters, Abigail and Hannah—
"Kind words are like honey, sweet to the soul and healing to the bones." (Proverbs 16:24) May you always walk with courage and compassion.

To my brothers—
for their loyalty, laughter, and the bond that outlasts distance.

To Angela—
whose grace under pressure reminded me what true leadership looks like.

And to my parents—
for teaching me that mercy and endurance are two sides of the same love.

CONTENTS

ACKNOWLEDGMENTS

This book could not have been written without the grace of God and the quiet faithfulness of those who stood beside me when the road was long and uncertain.

To my wife, Stephanie—your strength, patience, and courage are the steady rhythm beneath every word in these pages. You remind me daily what grace looks like when it walks around in skin.

To my daughters, Abigail and Hannah—your compassion and curiosity give me hope for the kind of world you'll help shape. You have taught me that faith is not inherited; it's discovered, lived, and tested in your own time.

To my brothers—whose laughter and loyalty continue to anchor me to the best parts of who I am. Thank you for showing me that even when paths diverge, family remains the truest compass.

To Angela—whose leadership in that jury room was as natural as it was courageous. You embodied integrity when it mattered most.

To Judge Daniel Hogan and the officers of the court—for modeling what humility looks like under the weight of authority.

To friends and colleagues who encouraged me to write when doubt whispered otherwise—your belief in this story helped me believe in its purpose.

To my parents—for the paradox of discipline and mercy that shaped me, and for showing me that faith is not the absence of struggle but the endurance through it.

Special thanks to Mr. Cory Goe for his gracious correspondence after reading this memoir. Our dialogue—rare between prosecutor and juror—was marked by mutual respect and a shared sense of calling. His words affirmed the purpose and hope at the heart of this book.

And finally, to the readers—thank you for giving your time and heart to this journey. My hope is not that you leave with answers, but that you walk away with courage—to wrestle, to believe, and to trust that grace still finds us in the fog between them.

Soli Deo Gloria.

AUTHOR'S NOTES

This book was never meant to be written. When the trial ended, I thought I could move on—file it away as another civic duty completed. But the experience did not leave quietly. It stayed with me, reshaping how I understood justice, mercy, and the quiet work of grace in ordinary lives.

What began as notes in the margins of memory became reflections about faith under pressure—how belief is tested not only in crisis, but in the long shadows that follow it.

I have learned that doubt is not the enemy of faith; it is the forge where faith is refined. The questions we carry do not disqualify us from belief—they invite us into it. Unreasonable doubt is not about certainty; it is about courage—the courage to keep seeking when clarity feels out of reach.

If you find yourself questioning, wondering, or even doubting as you turn these pages, you are not alone. Bring those doubts with you. Let's walk together.

All proceeds from this book will be donated to Christian faith-based ministries serving abused children, families in crisis, and those in prison.

May these pages stand as a quiet testimony to one enduring truth: Even in the shadow of unreasonable doubt, grace is still reason enough to believe.

—Gregg A. Stewart
Dublin, Ohio

PREFACE

"Be still, and know that I am God."

— Psalm 46:10 (ESV)

There's a moment before every story begins when silence carries more truth than speech. This is that moment.

I did not set out to write about doubt, or duty, or faith under pressure. I set out to tell the truth.

And sometimes, telling the truth means walking back through the long corridors of memory—the ones lined with echoes we thought we had already outgrown.

For me, those corridors led to a courtroom—a place where belief and reason, conviction and compassion, collided in a way I had never experienced before. I came to see that faith isn't proven in the bright hours when everything makes sense—it's refined in the shadows when nothing does.

This book is not about a verdict. It's about the quiet work of grace in the heart of a juror, and the God who sits beside us when judgment feels heavier than understanding.

This book began not as an idea but as a burden—a whisper that wouldn't let me rest. For a long time, I thought I had put that season of my life behind me. The trial, the questions, the doubt—it all felt settled, or at least quiet. But writing this book was like standing before a mirror I didn't think I needed to look into anymore. Every time I tried to turn away, something deeper kept urging: Someone needs to hear this.

I resisted at first. The story felt too personal, too raw. I told myself that time had already done its healing, that faith had already filled the cracks. But God, in His mercy, wasn't finished. What began as a courtroom experience slowly became a lesson in grace—a revelation that justice, mercy, and truth don't always meet neatly, but they always meet somewhere.

Along the way, I discovered that faith isn't the absence of doubt—it's the courage to keep walking when doubt joins the journey. Writing *Unreasonable Doubt* has reminded me that testimony isn't about perfection; it's about presence. It's about recognizing how God sends people—teachers, brothers, daughters, friends—to walk beside us when His voice feels faint.

My hope is that this book meets you where you are—not as a lecture but as a conversation between fellow travelers. If it helps you see that faith and reason, justice and mercy, doubt and belief can coexist within the same heart—then it has done what it was meant to do.

May these pages remind you that even in the silence, God is still speaking. And sometimes, the echo of His voice sounds a lot like our own.

PROLOGUE

I never expected to be called for a criminal trial involving the deepest and darkest sides of human suffering. Like many, I assumed my jury duty would amount to tedious hours spent deliberating a petty crime, not the harrowing allegations at the heart of *State of Ohio v. Muata M. Fisher.*

But as Juror Number Eight, I was thrust into a narrative that would challenge my faith, my convictions about justice, and my understanding of doubt.

The courtroom was new—large, formal, heavy with quiet reverence. Rows of polished leather chairs lined the gallery. Coming from the construction industry, my attention drifted instinctively toward the details: the millwork, the fit of the baseboards, the polish of the marble floors. Whoever built this place, I thought, took pride in their craft. Even the grout lines were straight. That small, unnoticed excellence steadied me. It was good to be reminded that some things in this world were still done with care.

Presiding from the bench was Judge Daniel Hogan, a man who looked as though he had stepped out of another century—tall, broad-shouldered, with a snow-white mustache and a patient gravity in his eyes. His presence filled the room, but not in an intimidating way. It was more like the calm authority of someone who had seen enough of the world to know what truly mattered.

He had a small ritual that caught my eye almost immediately—the careful way he unfolded his reading glasses, hinged in the middle rather than at the arms. He'd perch them on his nose, read a passage, then fold them again before setting them neatly back into his robe pocket. Every motion deliberate. Practiced. Reverent.

I remember looking around that courtroom and feeling the strange blend of dignity and dread that hangs over rooms like that. The air was cool, the light filtered through high windows, and everything seemed designed to remind us that what happened here mattered.

When the bailiff called us to stand, I felt the small but unmistakable weight of duty settle on my shoulders—the kind of weight that doesn't ask whether you're ready; it simply assumes you'll carry it.

Each of us filed into the jury box in silence. The sound of our footsteps echoed faintly against the marble floors. I took my seat—Juror Number Eight—and the sound of the wooden chair creaking beneath me felt louder than it should have. Across the room, the defendant sat at the table, still and watchful. His eyes moved slowly over the jurors as though memorizing each face, perhaps searching for one that looked merciful.

There's a particular quiet that comes when you realize your choices will affect someone's life forever. It isn't fear exactly—it's something deeper. A kind of holy unease.

I remember whispering a prayer I'd whispered a thousand times before, but never with such weight: "Lord, let me see the truth and give me the courage to follow it."

It's easy to talk about justice in the abstract. It's different when it sits across the room from you, wearing a suit and a nervous heartbeat.

In that moment, I wasn't thinking about faith or destiny. I was thinking about how fragile we all are—how quickly one decision, one accusation, one moment, can change the course of a life.

Chapter 1
FOUNDATIONS OF FAITH

Every belief begins somewhere. Before a courtroom, before the long nights of doubt and prayer, there were the voices that shaped me—the soil that steadied me.

My parents could not have been more different. My father—confident, boisterous, endlessly capable—and my mother—gentle, grounded, steadfast in her faith. Their marriage was both a meeting of worlds and a quiet collision of them.

He was gifted in nearly everything he touched—athlete, musician, mechanic, inventor—and for many people, he was a kind of local hero. The kind of man who could fix a motor in the afternoon, sing a hymn beautifully by evening, and tell a story that filled every room with laughter. But he was also a man shadowed by contradictions—raised in the church but later drifted, his discipline precise yet his temper unpredictable, his grace reserved mostly for those outside the home.

Growing up, I learned early that the same hands that could build could also bruise. For all his strengths, my father lived as if mercy were a luxury, not a duty. He used to say, "You won't find sympathy here. You'll find it in the dictionary—somewhere between shit and syphilis." It was his way of hardening us for the world, and maybe, in his own way, protecting us from it.

My mother, on the other hand, was pure resilience wrapped in grace. The eldest of seven, she had known hardship long before she ever knew comfort. She grew up under the shadow of an abusive, alcoholic father, and perhaps that's why faith became her refuge—not her inheritance. When she married my father, she was sixteen, stepping from the rural hills into a new kind of life she could hardly have imagined.

Later, when my father was stationed overseas during the war, she followed him to Japan—a young girl who had once ridden a half-blind pony to school, now navigating a foreign land where she was often treated as an unwelcome stranger. There, she gave birth to her first son, Stephen—a child who lived only six weeks. She flew home alone on a cargo plane, sitting beside a small casket. That image, even now, humbles me—the quiet endurance of a faith that refuses to die, even when everything else does.

She told us later that for years there was no money for a headstone, and that omission weighed on her spirit. It wasn't until many years later, when my brothers and I were grown, that we saved enough to buy one together. I think that stone stood for more than a name—it marked her perseverance, her dignity, and the restoration of something my father's practicality had long postponed.

Our home was not without love, but it was a love that had to make room for both discipline and survival. Except for the poker nights there was no alcohol inside our house—no profanity, either. My mother wouldn't have tolerated it. "Prayer is the first act of faith," she'd say. And somehow, even in the noise of my father's friends and their weekend card games, that truth held steady like a quiet hymn playing beneath it all.

The House of Collisions

Looking back, I think our home was a place where beauty and brokenness were always colliding—faith pressed up against frustration, laughter tangled with silence.

When my brothers and I were young, we didn't talk about the tension; we built around it. At night, while my father's friends built pyramids from beer cans on the same kitchen table, my brother and I built card houses from the leftover decks. We'd stay up until dawn, stacking and balancing until one of us exhaled too loudly and the whole thing collapsed. Then we'd start again.

Those quiet hours taught me something about endurance—and maybe about grace. You keep rebuilding, even when the structure falls apart, because that's what love demands.

Years later, my brother and I still build together, only now it's chess instead of cards. We start our games late at night, and even now, in the hum of our separate houses, the rhythm feels the same. My brother knows the openings by heart—solid, disciplined, deliberate. I favor the middle game—improvisational, full of motion, trying to see patterns unfold before they're visible. Together, we've found we can beat opponents that neither of us could conquer alone.

Maybe that's what faith is like—part memory, part movement, part mystery. One of us steady, the other restless, both needing each other to reach what we couldn't on our own.

I've come to think of life that way—as a long, imperfect game played between certainty and grace. My father's voice still echoes in me: "Make sure you deserve your place on the field." But my mother's voice is louder now: "Pray first, son. Pray first."

It reminds me of a scene from *Master Harold . . . and the Boys*, a play I first read in college. There's a moment when the characters talk about the beauty of dance—a world where people move without bumping into each other. I've never forgotten that line. Later in life, I even drove to Cincinnati just to see it performed on stage. Watching it, I remembered the scene where Sam takes the boy to the beach to fly a kite—to help him forget the shame of carrying his drunken father out of a bar.

I knew that pain. I'd been that boy—too young to enter the bar but old enough to go inside and lead my father home while my mother waited in the car.

And yet, like that play, my story isn't just about collisions—it's about grace that somehow finds room to move among them. Maybe that's what faith really is: not the absence of collisions, but the courage to keep dancing anyway.

Chapter 2

WHEN THE CALL OF DUTY BECOMES A TEST OF FAITH

"My Father, if it be possible, let this cup pass from me; nevertheless, not as I will, but as you will."

— Matthew 26:39 (ESV)

It was a cool November morning when I stepped from the sidewalk toward the Delaware County Courthouse. That mix of duty and apprehension pressed in on me—the weight of obligation colliding with the small comforts of Ohio in the fall. The air was sharp with the scent of drying leaves and faint woodsmoke, the kind of air that makes you stand a little straighter and breathe a little deeper.

The courthouse itself was impressive—a newer colonial-style building of white columns and red brick standing just off the square in Delaware, Ohio. It was stately but not cold. Orderly, but not unwelcoming. The kind of place that seemed to whisper of justice and consequence in the same breath. Beds of yellow mums lined the walkway, maples blazed orange above them, and the flag out front flicked lazily in the wind. I paused for a moment on the steps, trying to shake the feeling that I was walking into something more than civic duty—something appointed.

Inside, security greeted me with brisk professionalism. There was the usual X-ray machine and metal detector, but the tone was nothing like the sterile rush of an airport. Here, people looked you in the eye. The officers smiled—real smiles—and spoke with the quiet assurance of men and women who took their jobs seriously without taking pleasure in authority. One of them nodded me through with a simple, "Good morning, sir," and for a moment I felt less like an anonymous citizen and more like an invited participant in something important.

Once inside, I was directed to the jury assembly room where roughly forty others waited, scattered across rows of chairs. The atmosphere was subdued—half resignation, half curiosity. Some thumbed absently through their phones, others stared at the muted TV on the wall. You could sense the quiet hum of collective inconvenience—people pulled from their routines, all wondering how long this would take.

Coming from the construction industry, my attention drifted instinctively toward the details—the millwork, the fit of the baseboards, the polish of the marble floors. Whoever built this place, I thought, took pride in their craft. The banisters were smooth beneath the hand, the doorframes squared and tight. Even the grout lines were straight. That small, unnoticed excellence steadied me. It was good to be reminded that some things in this world were still done with care.

At the front of the room stood Johnie, the jury orientation attendant, who instantly struck me as someone who loved her work. There was a kindness to her—the kind that didn't come from training or policy, but from the heart. She answered every question with patience and humor, guiding us through the paperwork, calming the anxious, keeping the process human. In a place that could have felt cold or bureaucratic, she was a quiet anchor.

I filled out my forms and settled in, alternating between checking work emails and letting my thoughts wander. Like most people there, I assumed I'd be dismissed by noon. Maybe a petty theft, a minor dispute—a morning of inconvenience before heading back to the real world.

Around me, fragments of conversation drifted through the stillness. One woman murmured, "I just can't stand hearing about these kinds of cases," to no one in particular. Another leaned toward her neighbor, whispering, "You'd think something like this wouldn't happen here." Their words lingered—a reminder that even in a courthouse, people carry their private judgments in with them.

About an hour later, Johnie appeared again with a handful of sticky notes. When she reached me, she smiled and handed me one marked with a single number: 8. I slipped it into my pocket without thinking, unaware that number would follow me for the rest of the week—and, in some ways, for the rest of my life.

We were eventually called to the courtroom—a long, echoing walk down polished corridors lined with portraits of judges and clerks past. The air grew quieter with each step, reverent even. When we entered, I was struck by how still it felt. High ceilings, walls paneled in dark wood, everything gleaming faintly with lemon oil. It was beautiful in that understated way that made you instinctively lower your voice.

Presiding from the bench was Judge Daniel Hogan, a man who looked as though he had stepped out of another century—tall, broad-shouldered, with a snow-white mustache and a patient gravity in his eyes. His presence filled the room, but not in an intimidating way. It was more like the calm authority of someone who had seen enough of the world to know what truly mattered. I noticed, even then, the small ritual that would become familiar over the coming days: the careful way he'd unfold his reading glasses, perch them on his nose, read a passage, then fold them again before setting them neatly back into his robe pocket. Every movement was deliberate—practiced, reverent, even pastoral in its rhythm.

When he spoke, his voice carried a kind of warmth that made you want to listen. He began by reminding us that we were about to take part in one of the cornerstones of American justice—the trial by jury. "The attorneys are advocates," he explained. "I serve as referee. But you—the jurors—you are the decision-makers. Yours is a sacred duty."

He spoke about the presumption of innocence, about the obligation to weigh only the evidence presented, and about the standard of reasonable doubt as our guide. Then he paused, looking slowly across the room. "In criminal trials," he said, "circumstantial evidence is to be given the same consideration as direct evidence." He emphasized it twice, almost gently, as though he knew the concept might be hard to accept.

One instruction surprised me: no note-taking allowed. I've spent a lifetime documenting things—job sites, schedules, quotes, orders—and the idea of remembering days of testimony without notes felt impossible. But the judge's explanation stayed with me. "You must be fully present," he said. "Not just hearing words, but listening—absorbing, remembering. Justice depends not on what you write, but what you understand."

"Know this, my beloved brothers: let every person be quick to hear, slow to speak, slow to anger."
— James 1:19 (ESV)

At the time, I didn't realize how wise that instruction was. Later, during deliberations, when memories and impressions collided, it became clear that the absence of written notes forced us to rely on collective recall—not on whose handwriting seemed most convincing.

The questioning of potential jurors began. Some asked to be excused—one woman trembling as she said she couldn't handle a case involving children. Another man, nearly deaf, admitted he'd miss too much to serve fairly. Each was dismissed with understanding. Slowly, the field narrowed.

When it came my turn, I answered honestly—about my background, my faith, my work, my family. Wife Stephanie; two daughters, Abigail (12) and Hannah (9). My views on alcohol. Then came the moment that would decide my fate as Juror Number Eight. The prosecutor—Cory Goe, the Special Victims Chief—asked a question about circumstantial evidence versus direct evidence. "Does anyone here think it's unfair that the law treats those two as equal?"

There was a murmur in the room. When it reached me, I said, "It really doesn't matter what I think. If that's the law, and the judge says that's how we're to proceed, then that's how we should proceed."

I wasn't trying to sound righteous. It was simply what I believed—that obedience to authority and respect for law were part of the order God established. But afterward, the prosecutor nodded almost imperceptibly, and later I learned that moment had secured my seat among the twelve.

> "Let every person be subject to the governing authorities. For there is no authority except from God."
> — Romans 13:1 (ESV)

At the defense table sat the accused—Mr. Fisher—a man of imposing size, easily the largest in the room. His build fit his profession: a prison security guard, broad-chested, muscular. Yet there was a heaviness in his demeanor, a stillness that seemed born of resignation or calculation—I couldn't tell which. The defense attorney beside him was sharp, composed, his partner less so—nervous, awkward, fidgeting with his folders. I remember thinking that in a case like this, one that would hinge so much on the testimony of a young girl, a gentler voice might have served him better.

When the judge began to read the charges, the entire courtroom seemed to tighten. It was as if the very air recoiled from the words about to be spoken. I'd sat in courtrooms before—as a citizen, a student of the law, even as a curious observer—but nothing could have prepared me for the stillness that fell when he began.

His voice was calm, deliberate, and heavy with the weight of procedure. But beneath that legal cadence, I could hear something deeper—the echo of human brokenness written into every syllable.

"*The State of Ohio versus Muata M. Fisher...*"

"Count One: Rape of a minor, in violation of Section 2907.02..."

"Count Two: Gross sexual imposition..."

"Count Three: Corruption of a minor..."

Each charge landed like a blow. I remember glancing toward the defendant, then toward the gallery, and then toward the other jurors—strangers who, for the next four days, would become a kind of moral family. I could see the unease ripple through us as the words sank in. The language of the law is clinical, but its meaning is not. Behind each charge, nine in total, stood a story, and behind that story, a life forever marked.

It wasn't just the nature of the accusations that unsettled me; it was the realization that, for reasons known only to God, I was being asked to help discern truth in a case that touched the deepest wounds of the human condition.

At that moment, the courtroom no longer felt like a civic institution. It felt like a sanctuary turned battlefield—a place where truth and mercy would soon meet, and I was being asked to stand somewhere in between.

A quiet prayer rose in me, unbidden: "Lord, Thank You for the shelter of Your protection. Guard my girls from evil and give me strength to face what I must hear."

The judge's voice continued, but I barely heard it. I only knew, in that moment, that what I had assumed would be a routine civic duty had become something far more serious—a moral and spiritual test.

I thought of Paul's words:

> "Therefore, my beloved, as you have always obeyed, so now, not only as in my presence but much more in my absence, work out your own salvation with fear and trembling, for it is God who works in you, both to will and to work for his good pleasure."
> — Philippians 2:12–13 (ESV)

As those charges echoed in the quiet courtroom, I understood, maybe for the first time, what fear and trembling really meant—not terror, but reverence; not doubt, but awe at the weight of what was being asked of us.

And as I sat there, Juror Number Eight, I couldn't shake the sense that none of us were here by accident.

For Such a Time as This

"And who knows whether you have not come
to the kingdom for such a time as this?"
— Esther 4:14 (ESV)

By God's providence, I had the house to myself that week. With Stephanie and the girls away at Cedar Point, I spent the night in prayer and contemplation. The quiet emptied the house of distraction and filled it with the sense of responsibility I carried. Alone, I reflected on the solemn duty ahead, committing the process to God and praying that I would glorify Him in what was to come.

There was one person I would have loved to call at that moment: my older brother. He's a devout Christian—a genuine Bible scholar who, impressively, has committed the entire book of Romans to memory, word for word. Just two years older than me, he's been my protector since our earliest days, often standing between my father's harsh discipline and the rest of our family. From the start, he was gifted—a natural athlete, but even more, a young man marked by a serious, early faith that made him seem wise beyond his years. I was a less serious Christian through much of our youth. Only later did he begin to sharpen my theology, not by dogmatic prodding, but with patient questions and quiet logic.

I also have a younger brother, twelve years my junior—a retired police lieutenant and a man of deep faith, though of a very different temperament. Outgoing, decisive, and full of humor, he's always had a way of bringing light into any room he enters. Between the three of us, I suppose I'm the Goldilocks brother—less academic than one, less exuberant than the other. Somewhere in between, trying to bridge conviction with calm.

Then there's my mother—the kindest person I've ever met. We didn't have much growing up, but what we lacked in means she more than made up for in grace. She taught her three boys to love the Lord and to see His hand in all things. That foundation has stayed with me my whole life. Even now, I can still hear her voice when I'm wrestling with something heavy: "Pray, honey. Just pray." It's advice I've never outgrown.

Morning came early—five-thirty, earlier than my usual six—but sleep had not offered much rest. My body was taut with anticipation, my mind brimming with Scripture and responsibility. I followed my normal routine almost by reflex: a brief workout, an early run to clear my head, then a breakfast of fruit, yogurt, and granola. A hot shower, clean clothes, and I was out the door before the sun crested the horizon. I left early—much earlier than needed for a nine-o'clock arrival—but I wanted time in the parking lot to gather my thoughts. No radio that morning; instead, I filled the car with quiet prayer.

As I drove, my mind returned to the prosecutor's opening statement from the day before. Cory Goe had quoted Graham Greene: "There is always one moment in childhood when the door opens and lets the future in." He said that for Abby, the victim in the case, that door had opened far too early.

That line hit me hard—like a punch to the chest. I thought of my own childhood, and of the sudden, unwelcome ways that door had opened for me, too. My father's drinking, the confusion and instability it brought—it all came back in a rush. And then my thoughts turned to my own daughters, twelve and nine. I found myself wondering, almost defensively, *When will that door open for them?* Not if, but when. Because every parent knows—it always does.

As the car turned down Sandusky Street toward the courthouse, I remembered Romans 8:28:

> "And we know that in all things God works for the good of those who love Him, who have been called according to His purpose."

It's a verse I believe deeply—but one I've learned to use sparingly. When people are still hurting, that verse can land like a bandage on a wound that hasn't been cleaned yet. Sometimes what's needed isn't explanation but presence—the kind that listens and simply stays.

Still, I couldn't shake the feeling that God was working something out here, in me, even in this uncomfortable place between duty and faith. Deuteronomy 29:29 reminds us, "The secret things belong to the Lord our God, but the things revealed belong to us and to our children forever." That verse has always given me peace. Some mysteries are His alone to hold. Ours is simply to walk faithfully through the ones He reveals.

Arriving at the courthouse, my perception of it had changed. The mirror-polished marble floors and finely crafted millwork no longer felt extravagant; they felt right. The courthouse was the visible symbol of order against the chaos outside—a building both beautiful and burdened with purpose. Even the smell of lemon oil and old paper carried weight now.

The staff greeted me with familiar courtesy. Johnie, ever the steady presence, managed to set both tone and tempo with her gentle warmth. The deputies nodded, polite but alert. I noticed how everything in this place operated with quiet precision, like a liturgy of civic duty.

When I checked in, I thought briefly of Stephanie and the girls. The night before, when we spoke, we hadn't talked about the trial at all—just the normal things. That's one of the gifts of our marriage: She never pries. She just listens, supports, and lets me process things in my own time. Before we hung up, I asked her—as I often do—to keep an extra-close eye on the kids at the park. Not in a fearful way, just my usual gentle nudge: Have fun, but be safe. It's something I say often, but that night, the words carried a deeper echo.

As court began, I once again found myself studying Judge Hogan. His presence commanded the room—not by volume, but by steadiness. One small detail had first caught my attention: his reading glasses hinged in the middle, folding inward like a carpenter's rule. Every time he opened or closed them, there was a deliberate rhythm to it—an almost meditative gesture that punctuated his words. Each time he folded them, it was as though the courtroom collectively inhaled, waiting for what would come next.

The day's testimony turned heavier. The prosecution began laying out the narrative of Abby's early life. She had moved into Mr. Fisher's home at six years old—barely able to read, unable to recite the alphabet. It was astonishing to me that a child from such a background could even be enrolled in a district as rigorous as Westerville's. I thought about our own girls in Olentangy Schools—the flashcards, the sight words taped to walls, the countless evenings Stephanie spent helping them sound out words. I couldn't imagine how a child like Abby, without that foundation, could ever catch up. And yet, she had.

That was one of the things that struck me most about the case—not just the tragedy, but the paradoxes. Here was a man—Mr. Fisher—a prison guard, disciplined, imposing, part of a churchgoing family, taking in a daughter he hadn't known existed. And here was his wife, welcoming that child into her home, with two nearly grown children of her own. The situation defied easy logic, and yet they had done it. Against every expectation, Abby's grades improved, her reading soared, and by all outward appearances, she was thriving.

How could such goodness and such evil be alleged to coexist in the same house? That question haunted me as the prosecution recounted how Abby's accusations had emerged: first a physical confrontation about a school project, then a friend's encouragement to speak up, then the flood of allegations that followed. There was an ache in my chest as I listened—a father's ache, a juror's uncertainty, a believer's plea for truth.

The defense, for their part, tried to plant small seeds of doubt—timelines, inconsistencies, the natural flaws in memory.

He said something that stayed with me long after: "You will hear things that make you uncomfortable. You will see gaps in memory, contradictions in words. You may find yourself wishing for clearer evidence. That's not your failure—that's the human condition."

He paused, then added, "The burden is not on this man to prove his innocence. It's on the State to prove his guilt—beyond a reasonable doubt."

The phrase echoed. It was familiar from the judge's instructions, but in that moment, it carried a moral charge that went deeper. Beyond a reasonable doubt.

The line between faith and doubt has always fascinated me. In Scripture, doubt isn't always the enemy of faith; sometimes it's the crucible that strengthens it. But in court, doubt has its own sacred function—the protection of the innocent.

I thought of Thomas touching the wounds of Christ, of Job demanding answers he'd never fully receive. Maybe "reasonable doubt," in both faith and justice, isn't the absence of belief but the humble recognition that we see in part.

And there was something else, a quiet undercurrent that wasn't fully developed but lingered in the background: that Ms. Miller, Abby's biological mother, had petitioned to regain custody after getting her life together. The lawyers mentioned it briefly, almost awkwardly, as if they didn't quite know what to do with it. But I heard it. And it stayed with me.

When court adjourned that evening, I drove home in silence. The sun was low, the trees along the road flashing gold and red. The quiet gave me room to think—and to pray.

And I did.

I prayed not for answers, but for trust—that whatever mysteries God was working out in that courtroom, and in me, He would, in His time, make known.

Still, as I drifted toward sleep, one thought lingered. Somewhere in the tangle of testimony was that passing mention of custody—Ms. Miller's petition to regain her daughter after rebuilding her life. This serious felony trial was taking place in the middle of a custody suit. The defense hadn't pressed it, but it hung there like a loose thread.

I didn't know what to make of it yet. But I knew it mattered.

Chapter 3
WHO SINNED

"And his disciples asked him, 'Rabbi, who sinned, this man or his parents, that he was born blind?'"

— John 9:2 (ESV)

Abby Takes the Stand

When Abby took the stand, she was twelve—and mature beyond her years. She was very composed. Though what she described had taken place years earlier, when she was six, maybe seven, maybe eight. She couldn't remember exactly. That uncertainty itself was telling. Time had blurred the edges of memory, and her words carried both the simplicity of a child and the distance of someone trying to recall a story long rehearsed.

She didn't cry or show anger. Her voice was even, her answers short but clear. She didn't seem fearful or defensive—just steady, almost detached, as if she had found a way to tell what happened without having to feel it.

What stood out most to me was what was missing. There was no hatred in her words. No bitterness. In fact, there was still a softness when she spoke of her father. It wasn't affection exactly, but it wasn't anger either. It was something in between—an absence that felt like presence.

And that's what I couldn't get past. I couldn't find hate where the alleged victim hadn't even found anger. If she, the one most wronged, still seemed to hold some measure of care or confusion about her father, what right did I have to hate him in her place?

That was when my frustration began to shift. If I couldn't find certainty in her emotion, I turned my scrutiny to the process—the investigation itself. How could we be asked to decide something so severe when the evidence left so many holes? How could a child's quiet composure be weighed against an investigation that seemed careless at best? That tension stayed with me through every phase of the trial—the quiet conflict between faith in justice and doubt in men's ability to carry it out.

The testimony had taken its toll on everyone in the courtroom. Each word carried the weight of two realities: what might have happened, and what could never be proven beyond all doubt. There were moments when I caught myself studying her face, searching for some outward trace of anger or defiance. But it wasn't there. Her composure wasn't indifference; it was something else—a quietness that spoke of both love and pain. I remember thinking that kind of silence can unsettle a man who believes in justice, because it asks for mercy before it gives clarity.

The defense pressed the custody battle hard, trying to convince us that the case was less about abuse and more about leverage—a daughter caught in a family feud, a pawn in a struggle for control. And in a case where so much depended on he said, she said, that argument had power.

But as I listened, something deeper took root. She had said she still loved her father. That statement alone became a turning point in my mind. I believed her. I believed she did love him, and that love, fragile as it was, somehow made her testimony more credible, not less.

She was frail, yes, but she wasn't naïve. She was old enough to understand what her words meant—that if her father was convicted, he would spend much of his life in prison. And I could not bring myself to believe that she would invent such a story merely to change her living circumstances. Love, real love, carries too heavy a cost for deceit.

And that, in the end, was why I believed her. The love she bore for the one accused of harming her was impossible to reconcile in human terms, yet unmistakably genuine. It reminded me of something sacred—that even broken love can bear witness to truth.

Paul wrote, "And now these three remain: faith, hope, and love. But the greatest of these is love." That verse took on new weight for me during that trial. Because love, even wounded and bewildered, still reflects the image of the One who made it.

And perhaps that's why her frailty stayed with me. Because I've come to believe that the most powerful work God ever did was in the frailty of His Son. The world mistook that weakness for defeat, but it was the very strength that redeemed it. In that courtroom, I saw a glimpse of that same paradox—truth revealed not through certainty, but through suffering; not through power, but through love.

I still don't pretend to understand why some lives seem to begin under the shadow of suffering. From the start, it felt as though Abby never had a fair chance—born into brokenness, handed from one uncertainty to another. Yet even there, in that mystery, I've come to see what Jesus meant when He said the man was born blind "that the works of God might be displayed in him."

Maybe that's what faith means—not making sense of it all, but believing that even in the places that seem forsaken, God is still at work. Somehow, through a story that began in pain, His glory can still break through.

Author's Reflection – The Silence Between Anger and Love

There are moments in life when justice stands still, waiting for mercy to speak. The law can determine what is right, but only love can reveal what is true. The girl's quiet grace forced me to confront that difference. Her restraint wasn't denial—it was endurance. It was the kind of love that refuses to surrender to hatred, the kind that bears pain rather than multiplies it.

I've thought of her often since then. Not because of what she said, but because of what she didn't. In her silence, I learned that truth doesn't always shout. Sometimes it simply refuses to run.

Chapter 4
THE DELIBERATION

That morning, as all twelve of us assembled before going into the courtroom, a juror named Angela asked quietly, "Would it be alright if I opened us with a prayer?"

No one objected. We bowed our heads.

As she began praying, I prayed silently as well. I asked God that it would be a sincere, godly prayer—not an abstract invocation, but one directed to Him. And it was. Her prayer was simple and genuine. She asked God for wisdom, unity, clarity, and fairness, and that we would do what was right before Him.

When she finished, I felt a sense of calm and clarity. In that moment, I knew what I needed to do when the time came.

We then entered the courtroom, received the judge's final instructions, and were sent back to the deliberation room to begin.

The courtroom had felt solemn, almost sacred. The jury room, by contrast, felt like a utility closet that had been repurposed for justice. The air was stale. The table was too small for twelve adults, and the chairs creaked every time someone shifted their weight. Gone were the carved wood panels and high ceilings of the courtroom. Here, under buzzing fluorescent lights, the veneer of order peeled away.

This was where the real trial began—not for the defendant, but for each of us.

The door clicked shut, and for a moment there was silence—twelve people breathing in the same nervous air. It was a strange kind of intimacy. I could almost hear the weight of the verdict waiting on the other side of the walls.

Before anyone could settle too deeply into the tension, I stood. "We'll need a foreman," I said, trying to sound steady but not controlling. "I'd like to nominate Angela."

She looked startled, then smiled—one of those quiet, gracious smiles that disarm a room. "Only if no one objects," she said.

No one did. It wasn't just relief that made everyone nod; it was something about her presence. Angela wasn't loud or commanding. She was composed, calm, and unflinchingly fair. Dark hair framed her face, her eyes alert but kind. She had that rare gift of making people feel heard without saying much at all. Later, she told me that my nomination caught her off guard—but in that moment, it felt providential.

Once Angela accepted, I stood again, this time picking up the dry-erase markers and eraser from the tray. I've always believed that every meeting—whether in business, church, or a jury room—ought to start with the end in mind. Stephen Covey wrote that principle years ago, and it stuck with me. I've told people for decades that before you start, you should ask, "What do we want to have accomplished before we close?"

So that's what I did.

I uncapped the marker and wrote our goals on the whiteboard:

- Follow the judge's instructions and decide the case based solely on facts, without prejudice or sympathy.
- Maintain the presumption of innocence.
- If we make a mistake, let it be freeing a guilty man—not convicting an innocent one.

Then, without meaning to sound sanctimonious, I added my personal goals beneath. "I want to honor God in this process," I said quietly. "To glorify Him through honesty and fairness. To listen—truly listen—to others. And to seek justice, love mercy, and walk humbly."

Someone—her voice soft but firm—added, "Nothing left unsaid." We all nodded. That one struck home.

When we went around the table sharing first impressions, it didn't take long to realize I was the outlier. Eleven people saw guilt as clear as glass. Only one didn't.

Still, there was civility at first. I could feel their curiosity about my hesitance, even respect. I told them I didn't mind being challenged—that I'd rather be proven wrong honestly than convinced falsely. But as the hours wore on, patience began to thin. The explanations came quickly—some reasonable, others exasperating.

"I just know."

"His wife was too emotional."

"He thinks he's above the law."

"My family says I'm clairvoyant."

"I sympathize with Abby."

And my favorite: "Some people still think O.J. is innocent."

Angela intervened gently, bringing the group back to focus when it drifted toward mockery. Her tone never sharpened. If anything, she steadied the air around her.

At one point, I raised the uncomfortable question of possible racial bias. It wasn't an accusation, just an acknowledgment of how perception can shape justice. The only Black juror quickly said he didn't believe that it was at play and that he was convinced of the defendant's guilt. Angela caught my eye then—grateful, I think, that someone had voiced what she hadn't dared to. Later, she told me she was married to a Black physician and that my willingness to broach the subject reminded her of him—analytical, principled, maybe a little too persistent. We both laughed at that.

Judge Hogan's instructions were to decide without prejudice or sympathy. I felt that was a good enough answer to deal with the questions I had regarding racial bias. However, when I mentioned without sympathy, there was not a good response to that. I could certainly understand that. My heart broke for the whole family. However, given the judge's instructions, I couldn't let emotion influence my decision.

Through it all, I felt both isolated and anchored—anchored by conviction, but aware of how easily conviction can harden into pride. Ours was a sacred process, and I prayed silently more than once. My goal wasn't to win an argument; it was to leave that room knowing I had honored God with honesty. As the discussion grew more strained, one comment in particular shifted the room. A juror challenged me sharply, suggesting that my hesitation meant

I didn't believe Abby at all. Before I could respond, Angela spoke up—calmly, clearly, and without taking sides.

"He's not saying he doesn't believe her," she said. "He's saying he's not certain yet."

The tension in the room eased just slightly. Her words gave me the space I needed—not to argue, but to think, to pray, and to keep working through the evidence with honesty. I could have hugged her in that moment. She had understood my heart before I had fully articulated it myself.

Angela helped keep that space open for me. I didn't realize then how much her grace would matter later, when I'd begin to feel betrayed by how things unfolded.

At one point, I asked if we could review a portion of Abby's video testimony. Everyone agreed, and the bailiff brought in the equipment. I took the remote and played the section I felt we needed to revisit—one where her statements clearly contradicted themselves. It wasn't subtle. It was the kind of inconsistency anyone listening carefully would recognize.

When the contradiction appeared, I waited.

Five seconds.

Ten.

Fifteen.

No one acknowledged it.

I let the video run a little longer, hoping someone would speak. But the silence held. It wasn't hostility; it was avoidance. And yet, earlier we had agreed on one of our guiding principles: *nothing left unsaid.* And here we were, letting something important pass without a word.

Finally, I paused the video.

"I need to say something," I said. "We agreed nothing would be left unsaid. What we just heard was a clear contradiction, and no one acknowledged it. I have to be honest—that makes me feel like I've lost your trust."

The room tightened. No one denied hearing it. They had heard it—they simply hadn't wanted to be the first to say it out loud.

Then Angela spoke—publicly, and without hesitation.

"I need to apologize," she said. "I heard it too. I knew I should have said something, and I didn't. We agreed nothing would be left unsaid, and I didn't speak up."

Her words weren't emotional or defensive. They were factual and honest, and they mattered more than she knew. They didn't erase the tension, but they restored truth to the room and reminded me that at least one person understood what I was experiencing.

Her apology didn't change the evidence, but it changed the air. It allowed me to stay grounded—not in stubbornness, but in integrity.

But the unity didn't last. As the first hour stretched into the second, the atmosphere shifted. What began as thoughtful discussion gradually slipped into impatience. Voices grew louder, chairs scraped, and pens tapped against the table. People began talking over one another. I recognized the dynamic from other settings—how quickly a group can move from careful reasoning to the assumption that certainty has already been reached.

I tried to listen more than speak and to pray between breaths. I wasn't angry; I was still searching. But I could tell my questions were wearing on them. I was the one point of hesitation in a room that wanted unanimity. And I knew that as long as my doubts remained, peace wouldn't.

Verdict and Reflection

That was when one of the men leaned forward, his voice tight with frustration. "What do you even mean by 'reasonable doubt'? How much doubt are we talking about? Give me a number."

The room went still. It was a fair question—simple, direct, and impossible. The words hung in the air like a challenge. All eyes turned to me. I took a breath.

"For me," I said, "beyond a reasonable doubt means I'm about ninety to ninety-five percent certain. That's the point where I could cast my vote without hesitation."

He shook his head, almost scoffing. "That's unreasonable."

He may not have meant it as a title, but it landed like one.

Still, the stakes felt too high to lower the bar. Someone's life, someone's freedom—hung on where we set that line. And the truth was, I couldn't let go of that tension. Not in that moment. Before I could respond, something in me went back years—to a place where I had once known what certainty felt like.

When I worked underground in the coal mines, danger was never theoretical. I had seen what happens when things go wrong—machines that chewed through rock like paper, and men who never came home the same. One of my closest friends had been in a catastrophic accident. I visited him in the hospital afterward. He had a grade-ten head injury, and though his speech was barely intelligible, he took my hand and whispered, "The hardest thing is I survived… and I know how bad I am." Those were the last words he ever spoke. Moments later he seized, and from then on, he was a quadriplegic.

Not long after that, I started working on Big Bill's section. Everyone called him that—he was built like a linebacker and was one of the best miners I ever knew. Early on I noticed something that could have cost him his life. Each of us carried a mine rescuer—a small, vacuum-sealed canister that, once the seal was broken, gave you about an hour of breathable air if there was a fire. One day I saw that Bill's seal had been cracked and duct-taped back together, probably from bumping against the wall. He didn't realize that his hour of safety had already expired. I walked him out of the mine myself to the safety office, and together we replaced his unit while they explained how serious that mistake could have been. From that day on, a bond formed between us that never wavered. We trusted each other implicitly.

So when that continuous miner jammed—a monster of a machine clogged with coal—and I had to crawl in to clear it, I didn't hesitate. They shut it down, and I climbed in, neck-deep in black dust and steel teeth. The only thing standing between me and death was Big Bill, guarding the switch. And I knew, beyond all question, that he would have died before letting anyone turn that machine back on.

That's what certainty felt like—the kind that leaves no room for doubt. And maybe that's why this case weighed on me the way it did. Because I'd seen what life and death really meant, and now I was watching a man's life hang in the balance again—only this time, it wasn't steel and coal that could crush him. It was us.

And that's what I was searching for in that jury room—something I could hold with that same kind of conviction. Because with Mr. Fisher's life in the balance, I didn't want to guess. I wanted to know.

As I reflected on the deliberations, the evidence, the testimony, and the meeting that followed, I remembered the agreement we committed to: In order to convict, we must be firmly convinced. I can say, without equivocation, that we were. And more than that, I believe this trial pursued truth with sacred deliberation. By God's grace, we did everything humanly possible to render a verdict that was just and right.

I kept thinking back to something Angela said in the deliberation room. When a juror accused me of not believing Abby, she corrected him gently: "He's not saying he doesn't believe her—he's saying he's not certain yet." At the time, I didn't realize how much that word—*certain*—would stay with me. It named something I hadn't been able to articulate. I had been searching for a kind of clarity the judge never required of us, a level of certainty that doesn't exist in this life. Faith, by definition, begins where certainty ends. Angela's phrasing clarified that for me in a way the instructions alone hadn't.

But as I prayed and thought about the judge's instructions—that our standard was to be "firmly convinced," not "absolutely certain"—I realized that kind of clarity wasn't coming. Not here. That level of certainty only comes from God.

So when the man across from me said I had "unreasonable doubt," I thought to myself: *Maybe he's right.* Later, I understood he wasn't wrong—but neither was I. Doubt isn't the absence of truth. Sometimes it's the doorway to it.

The whiteboard still held our goals, and I kept glancing back at them like a compass: Seek justice. Love mercy. Walk humbly with God. I had written those words myself, but now they felt like they were written for me.

He said his number was sixty to sixty-five percent. I knew that was the standard for an indictment—probable cause—not the measure for conviction. The difference mattered, but explaining it wouldn't have changed anything. By that point, logic had stopped serving the room. Clarity had become the enemy of consensus.

I remember thinking how fragile this process really is—how much it depends on the moral and intellectual readiness of those chosen to sit in judgment. John Adams once said our Constitution was made only for a moral and religious people, and I understood that line in a new way. The machinery of justice can't function without conscience at its center.

That realization humbled me more than it angered me. It reminded me that even reason, when separated from virtue, can lose its way.

As the afternoon waned, I could feel the strain tightening in the room. People were exhausted—mentally, emotionally, spiritually. The smell of stale coffee lingered. Someone rubbed their temples. Someone else stared blankly at the floor.

By now the judge's message had reached us: If we weren't close, we'd adjourn and return after the weekend. That's when one of the jurors slammed a hand on the table. "I can't come back Monday—I've got surgery!"

The room froze. There it was—the breaking point. Start over with alternates, or finish now.

I excused myself to the restroom and prayed for clarity. My prayer wasn't eloquent—just an earnest cry for wisdom and courage. Two paths lay before me: Hold firm and risk a hung jury, or yield my doubts and allow the process to conclude.

In that small courthouse restroom, I made a quiet bargain with God. I told Him that I could not take the risk of letting this man go free to face no justice at all. I would cast my vote for guilt—but I would not rest until I found peace about that decision.

At that moment, looking into the mirror, I knew exactly what I was doing. It was a solemn oath, not a passing prayer. I knew what it could cost me—everything I owned, every comfort my family had worked for, every plan we had made. And yet, I also knew Stephanie would understand. She is a rock. I knew that if God required the cost, she would shoulder it beside me without hesitation.

Chapter 5
THE VERDICT

When the jury finally returned to the courtroom, I knew my vote had not been born in that room alone. It had begun days earlier, when Abby spoke with a love that defied reason. I had carried that love with me into deliberations like a silent witness—a reminder that truth is sometimes carried by those too young to explain it and too brave to deny it.

Her frailty had not weakened her credibility; it had baptized it in something sacred. I believed her then, and that belief had shaped everything that followed. By the time the bailiff opened the door for our return, I was no longer wrestling with whether she loved her father—I was wrestling with what justice must look like when love and truth stand on opposite sides of the same testimony.

So there it was—the judge read the verdict: guilty of eight counts of child rape and one count of gross sexual imposition. The words fell heavy in the still air. The defendant didn't move.

Abby's mother covered her face and wept. I looked down at the table in front of me, trying to steady the weight that had settled somewhere between my heart and my conscience.

It is hard to describe that moment—the mixture of gravity, grief, and grace that descended all at once. I didn't feel triumphant or even resolved. I felt sorrowful. Because even when justice is done, it still breaks something sacred.

The courtroom emptied slowly, as though the world outside no longer moved at the same pace. The air felt thinner, quieter. The bailiff opened the door for us, and as I stepped into the hallway, the sound of footsteps echoed like a benediction—one of those moments when time seems to widen, and you realize you've crossed a threshold you can never quite return from.

Justice had spoken. But mercy was still whispering.

After the Verdict – The Invitation Back

Before we were dismissed for good, Judge Hogan and both attorneys invited us back into the courtroom to speak openly about the case. It wasn't a formality; it was an act of respect. They wanted to answer questions—to help us process the weight of what we had just carried.

The judge's tone was pastoral, the attorneys' candid. For the first time since the trial began, there was no procedure—just people, tired but sincere, reflecting on justice and mercy. Several jurors shared how difficult it had been, and a few said they appreciated my persistence, that it had helped them realize the gravity of what we were doing. Judge Hogan nodded and said something I've never forgotten:

"Deliberation isn't argument—it's conscience at work." In that room ours was.

It was during that conversation that I learned something that stayed with me. The defense attorney told us the defendant had passed a lie-detector test—a detail that, for legal reasons, had not been admissible in court. He also admitted that he hadn't raised several points he could have, including inconsistencies in the timeline and elements of the custody dispute, because he thought they might "muddy the waters" for the jury.

Hearing that explained the tension I had felt during deliberation—that I was seeing gaps in the defense that he himself had chosen not to fill.

That moment humbled me even more. The law had its boundaries; conscience had to live within them. But it also affirmed that the doubts I carried weren't signs of weakness—they were the cost of taking justice seriously.

After the Verdict – The Meeting

I had promised God that if I was not assured the process had been carried out as fairly as humanly possible, I would move heaven and earth to make it right. Everything I had—time, money, reputation—was already His, and I would spend it all if justice demanded it.

That is why, when I climbed those courthouse steps the following Tuesday morning to meet with the prosecutor and his assistant, my hands trembled. It was, once again, a morning of fear and trembling. I prayed I would not find what I was prepared to confront.

By God's grace, I didn't. I met men and women of integrity—people of faith, weary but sincere—and I left their office relieved beyond words.

They told me the story of Abby and how they had spent a lot of time interviewing and questioning her. I will not share those details here, but I was convinced there was no bias in the prosecutor's office or a racially motivated justice system. They even offered to meet with our church and school to discuss internet safeguards, the hazards of online predators, and their willingness to help our community.

I want to say something about Cory Goe and his assistant. They were not just professionals doing their jobs; they were men and women standing on the front lines for the vulnerable—the voiceless, the abused, the forgotten. Their calm resolve carried the quiet weight of people who fight battles most of us never see.

As I walked out of that meeting, gratitude and humility mingled in me. I had wrestled for a week with doubt, fear, and moral exhaustion. Cory Goe had been doing it for a lifetime. He never said it, but as I shook his hand, I could almost hear the question I knew God had once asked me in gentler ways:

Where were you, Gregg? You see people like this too.

That thought stayed with me. It didn't condemn—it commissioned. It reminded me that the call to justice doesn't end when the courtroom empties. For those like Cory Goe, it begins again every morning. And for me, it was a quiet conviction that I hadn't done my part—not yet.

That moment became another Ebenezer—a marker of humility and resolve. God had not only proven His faithfulness;

He had shown me the faithfulness of those He sends to bear His heart for the broken.

That moment was my dark night of the soul, and it ended not with revelation but with quiet mercy. God had tested the vow of my heart, and, like Abraham on the mountain, I walked away knowing He had provided the lamb.

So I placed my Ebenezer there—a stone of remembrance to the God who met me in fear and trembling and proved Himself faithful yet again. In that place, I learned that faith isn't measured by certainty, but by the willingness to trust when certainty is gone.

When I walked out of that meeting, I carried a quiet resolve. The weight of decision had not lifted, but it had settled—not in triumph, but in surrender. Whatever the outcome, I knew I had done what I believed was right before God.

And as I reflected on everything that had unfolded—the deliberations, the evidence, the testimony, and the meeting that followed—I remembered the judge's charge to us before we began: that to convict, we must be firmly convinced of the defendant's guilt.

And though the weight of that phrase stayed with me long after the trial, I can say without equivocation that I am firmly convinced of something else as well: that this trial was conducted with a sacred and deliberate pursuit of truth. I am firmly convinced that, by God's grace, we did everything humanly possible to render a verdict that was just and right.

In that conviction, there was no pride—only gratitude. Gratitude that justice, however imperfect, had been sought with integrity. Gratitude that mercy had not been forgotten. And gratitude that, somehow, grace had carried us all the way through.

Author's Reflection – Ill Fares the Land

"Ill fares the land, to hastening ills a prey,
Where wealth accumulates, and men decay."
— Oliver Goldsmith, 1770

He wrote those words more than two centuries ago, yet they sound as if they were written for us. Goldsmith wasn't simply mourning a village; he was mourning a conscience. He saw a world where abundance outpaced empathy, and where the measure of a nation shifted from the strength of its character to the size of its gain.

When I think back on that deliberation room—the tension, the fatigue, the fragile way truth trembled between us—I can't help but feel the same ache. It wasn't only about guilt or innocence; it was about something larger unraveling in real time: our ability to listen, to discern, to care.

That same erosion Goldsmith saw in his fields and cottages now hides in subtler places—in our conversations, our judgments, our hearts. We're growing richer in information but poorer in understanding, louder in opinion but quieter in compassion. We've learned how to win, but forgotten how to weep.

A society can survive disagreement, even injustice. What it cannot survive is the slow withering of the soul—when conscience grows comfortable and mercy grows rare. That's the decay that doesn't announce itself; it settles in quietly, disguised as progress.

Goldsmith's deserted village was overrun by wealth; ours risks being overrun by weariness. Yet even in that warning there is hope—because awareness is the first stirring of redemption.

Desolate ground can still bear fruit if it's turned by repentance and watered with grace.

Perhaps that's what a world without collisions truly is—not a perfect world, but a penitent one. A place where grace and justice, once at odds, finally learn to move in step, each giving the other room to pass.

Author's Reflection – Fear and Trembling

There are moments when obedience feels less like victory and more like surrender. I used to think faith meant confidence—that if I just prayed hard enough, clarity would come like light through stained glass. But I've learned that sometimes, faith is what remains when the glass stays dark.

The courtroom taught me that justice has limits, but grace does not. It reminded me that God's sovereignty doesn't erase our questions—it sanctifies them. And that even when we act with trembling hands, He judges not by our certainty, but by our sincerity.

When I left that courthouse for the last time, I didn't feel vindicated. I felt humbled. The weight of the verdict wasn't something to celebrate; it was something to carry. But in that carrying, I found what I had been searching for all along—not the assurance that I was right, but the peace of knowing He was present.

> "For it is God who works in you, both to will
> and to work for His good pleasure."
> — Philippians 2:13 (ESV)

And in that truth, I rested—not in understanding, but in trust.

A Child of Light Walking in Darkness

> "Who among you fears the Lord and obeys the voice of His servant? Let him who walks in darkness and has no light trust in the name of the Lord and rely on his God."
> — Isaiah 50:10 (ESV)

There are seasons when God withholds the light not to abandon us, but to strengthen us. Faith is not the absence of darkness—it's the courage to keep walking when sight is gone. I have learned that obedience in the dark often reveals the brightest kind of grace.

Reflective Interlude – Faith and Doubt

In the days that followed, I found myself caught in that quiet space between justice and mercy—where the noise of judgment fades, and the deeper questions begin.

Sometimes, when I'm talking with people about faith, they'll say, "I understand what you believe, but I just can't get there. I have too many doubts."

I usually tell them, I understand that. I've certainly been to the mountain with Peter, James, and John and have been made a witness to the glory of God at work in my life. The arc of my journey bears witness to His providence—the way He weaves purpose through events I never could have orchestrated myself.

But I've also been to that same mountain and found nothing but wilderness. I've had seasons when the canyon below was on fire, and I stood there watching it burn—everything I thought was secure, burned to the ground. I've cried out the same words John the Baptist once asked from his prison cell: "Jesus, are You the One who is to come, or shall we look for another?" That question isn't unbelief—it's the honest ache of a heart still searching for light in the dark. And yet, in time, when the flames finally quieted, I looked down and saw something unexpected. In the ashes, there was grace.

Once, as a reckless teenager, five of us shared one motorcycle and a bad idea—a ride out to an abandoned strip-mine quarry on a blistering summer day. We carried too many bottles of malt liquor and not nearly enough sense. The quarry was deep—coal country's forgotten wound, filled with cold water and danger.

After a few races to a small peninsula in the middle, I realized too late that I was too drunk and too tired to swim back. Halfway across, I felt my strength give out. Panic set in. The old saying is that you go down three times—I remember it clearly. On the third, as water filled my lungs, I saw the sun slipping away through the green water above me.

Then—darkness.

When I opened my eyes, I was on the bank, lungs burning, body torn by briars. My older brother, who hadn't been drinking, had pulled me from the water with the help of our friends. Grace had a pulse that day. I didn't earn it; it just found me.

Years later, there was a different kind of drowning. A quieter one. A season when the weight of responsibility and uncertainty pressed so heavily that faith itself felt like a distant echo. A friend met me in that darkness—not with preaching or persuasion, but with presence. He sat through long nights, said little, and simply stayed.

In time, the silence began to heal me. Until one night, I could finally whisper the prayer that had been waiting in my chest all along: "Lord, I believe; help Thou my unbelief."

Now I know that in those seasons when I thought God was absent, He was actually holding me in the palm of His hand. That's what grace is.

So when someone tells me they can't believe because they still have doubts, I tell them: Bring your doubt with you. Doubt isn't the enemy of faith—it's the crucible that strengthens it.

Like Philip said to Nathanael, "Come and see." Walk the road, even with your questions. Faith doesn't begin where doubt ends; it grows in the soil of it.

If you're certain, you don't need faith. Certainty can be measured and proven. Faith, by contrast, asks you to trust what you can't see—to hope when the evidence runs out. As Paul wrote in Romans 8:24–25 (ESV):

> "For in this hope we were saved. Now hope that is seen is not hope. For who hopes for what he sees? But if we hope for what we do not see, we wait for it with patience."

That verse reminds me that hope isn't proof—it's perseverance. And faith isn't the absence of doubt; it's the courage to move through it.

That, I suppose, is what unreasonable doubt really means. Not that faith ignores reason, but that faith dares to reach beyond it. It believes anyway. And in that space between belief and uncertainty, grace does its quiet work.

Because in the end, faith isn't the absence of questions—it's the presence of God in the silence that follows them. And in that silence, I learned that conviction is not swagger but stewardship.

Grace is often clearest when certainty burns away.

Chapter 6
IN LIGHT OF ETERNITY

Before the courthouse quieted in my memory, I kept returning to something Judge Hogan said early in the trial. He compared a jury to an ambulance.

"You see them every day," he told us. "They pass you on the road, sirens wailing, and you hardly take notice. But when you're the one in need—when it's your life on the line—suddenly that ambulance becomes the most important thing in the world. For a man on trial, the jury is his ambulance. It's what stands between him and injustice."

Those words stayed with me long after the verdict. But as I've reflected, I've come to believe something else too: Sometimes the law itself needs an ambulance. When justice becomes so procedural that it forgets its purpose—or when conscience is dismissed as inconvenience—it starts to lose its pulse. A jury isn't only there to rescue the accused; it's there to keep justice accountable, to remind the system that mercy and truth still matter.

Because when law operates without conscience, and justice goes unchecked by compassion, what follows isn't order. It's a quieter kind of lawlessness—one that hides behind the appearance of doing everything right.

I remember thinking how fragile this process really is—how much it depends on the moral and intellectual readiness of those chosen to sit in judgment. John Adams once said our Constitution was made only for a moral and religious people, and I understood that line in a new way. The machinery of justice can't function without conscience at its center.

I had learned by then that justice, standing alone, can be cold. It may win the argument, but it rarely heals the wound. I had also seen how mercy or grace, offered without clarity, becomes little more than confusion—compassion without direction, kindness detached from truth. And yet, I knew too that mercy without justice was its own form of injustice. That kind of grace—the kind that looks away from accountability—wasn't love at all. It was lawlessness dressed as virtue.

There's a strange relief that comes when your striving finally quiets. It doesn't mean all the answers have come—it just means you've stopped demanding them.

In those weeks after the trial, I began to sense that the greater lesson was never about a verdict at all. It was about surrender. About learning to let go of my need to reconcile every inconsistency and instead rest in the faithfulness of a God who sees the whole picture when I can only see in part.

I thought often of Paul's words in 1 Corinthians 13:12: "For now we see through a glass, darkly; but then face to face." That verse had always sounded poetic to me—until it became practical. The glass darkly was not a metaphor anymore; it was my life.

The older I get, the more I realize how much of faith is trust without full understanding. I once believed peace came from resolution. Now I believe it comes from relationship—from knowing the One who holds the answers even when He withholds them from me.

One night, lying awake long after the house had gone quiet, I thought about Abby again—about her courage, her composure, and the mystery of how grace finds its way even into trauma.

Somewhere between her strength and my surrender, I felt the faintest sense of peace—like the closing of a chapter, but not the end of the story.

Maybe that's the real work of faith—to keep living in the questions, trusting that one day, the answers will come in light.

"Now faith is the substance of things hoped for,
the evidence of things not seen."
— Hebrews 11:1

For the Christian, the final word is summarized perfectly in Ecclesiastes 12:13: "When all has been heard, the conclusion of the matter is this: fear God and keep His commandments, for this is the whole duty of man."

And as far as the trial goes, if someone were to ask what revelation I gained from that experience, I would agree with St. Augustine in *The City of God*: "There is enough justice in the world to be assured of God's providence; enough injustice to be assured of the necessity of God's final judgment."

We all live *coram Deo*—before the face of God. And as Peter reminds us, He is "the Father who judges impartially according to each one's deeds" (1 Peter 1:17).

And yet, that same God who judges perfectly is also the One who redeems completely. His justice restores; His mercy repairs. And perhaps that's where the story of faith always leads—not to the courtroom, but to the home.

Chapter 7
LEGACY AND REFLECTION

I used to think legacy was something you left behind. Lately, I've come to believe it's something you live—moment by moment, in the quiet decisions no one sees. Maybe that's what reflection really is: the act of tracing the light backward, to see where grace first began to shine through the cracks.

My father used to say, "You won't find sympathy here. You'll find it in the dictionary—somewhere between 'shit' and 'syphilis.'" It was one of those lines that landed somewhere between humor and hard truth. I was walking home from a tennis match I'd lost in the finals, still sulking, when he stopped me.

"Hold on," he said. "That sounds like you're looking for sympathy. That's a conversation for you and your mother to have. But I can tell you where to find it..." He grinned, then gave that line—half a joke, half a lesson.

At the time, I didn't know how much of him was in that sentence. He was teaching me not to expect comfort from a world that won't always give it. But I see now there was something else there—a strange kind of love, disguised as toughness. The kind of love that makes you stand up straighter after you've been knocked down. The kind that believes endurance is its own kind of grace.

For years, I thought my father and I spoke different languages. He spoke in challenges; my mother spoke in prayers. She'd whisper, "Pray, honey. Just pray." He'd bark, "Work harder." Or, sometimes, "Gird your loins."

But as I've grown older, I've realized they were both saying the same thing in different dialects of love. She taught me surrender. He taught me resilience. Together, they prepared me for a world that would demand both.

It's taken me most of a lifetime to see that their voices were never at odds; they were in concert. My mother's grace was the melody, my father's grit the harmony. And I needed both to carry me through the music of this life.

I think about that often—especially now. There's something about age and reflection that makes you see your parents not as figures in your story, but as people in their own right—flawed, scared, trying their best to love in ways they understood. I used to measure them by what they got wrong. Now I measure them by what they survived.

One of the first people to help me see that was Mrs. Crabtree, my English teacher. She handed me a worn copy of *The Grapes of Wrath* my sophomore year and said, "Take this home. Read it like it's a mirror." I didn't fully understand what she meant, but I did what she asked. That book changed the way I saw people—and the way I saw my father. Steinbeck's stories of dust and dignity, of men trying to hold their families together in the storm, gave me language for what I had only felt. It was the first time I realized my father's hardness might have been a kind of mercy—a way of keeping his own storms from blowing through us.

That book also gave us a bridge. He was a baseball man; I was a tennis player—worlds apart. But books pulled us back together. He loved reading, and soon we started reading the same books. On his sober nights, we'd sit side by side watching *King Kong* or *Godzilla*, talking about stories bigger than ourselves.

We started with Steinbeck—*The Grapes of Wrath*, *East of Eden*, *Of Mice and Men*, and his favorite, *Cannery Row*. Then we wandered into Russian literature—Ghosts by Ibsen, Lermontov, Pushkin, Dostoevsky. You name it. I still remember how we laughed out loud talking about Kafka's Gregor in *The Metamorphosis*.

We didn't always say much, but those moments gave us a language that love alone hadn't managed yet. They gave us common ground again. Even years later, our phone calls often began the same way: "What are you reading?"

It was a simple question, but beneath it was something deeper—his way of saying, *We're still connected.*

When I close my eyes, I can still hear the rhythm of their house: the scrape of a chair, the slam of a door, my mother humming while she cooked, the muffled laughter of my father's poker nights. It wasn't always peaceful, but it was alive.

And maybe that's the point of legacy—not perfection, but persistence. Not the absence of struggle, but the decision to stay in the story when walking away would be easier.

Looking back, I think my father was teaching me something my faith would later confirm—that love, real love, is not always soft. Sometimes it's the kind that corrects, the kind that risks being misunderstood, the kind that demands growth.

Maybe that's why grace means more to me now than it ever did before. You don't really appreciate mercy until you've needed it. You don't understand forgiveness until you've been forgiven.

Even now, when I hand my daughters a book or quote a verse, I think of him—and of that classroom where literature first met conscience. Stories have a way of binding generations together. They teach us, in their own quiet way, how to forgive the people who taught us courage the only way they knew how.

There are lessons that come like light breaking through clouds, and others that arrive like rain that doesn't stop. Both, I've learned, are grace.

When I look back now, I see how much of my faith was formed not by clarity but by collision—between what I believed and what I saw, between what I hoped for and what hurt me. And through it all, grace kept showing up: in courtrooms, in doubt, in the small mercies of ordinary people.

Maybe that's the legacy I want to leave behind—not certainty, but faithfulness. Not spotless belief, but the willingness to believe again after everything's been tested.

And as for reflection—well, I suppose it's not just about looking back. It's about seeing how every hard thing, every confusing season, every unanswered prayer has been slowly redeeming something in you.

When I think of legacy now, I don't picture trophies, or verdicts, or even the stories people might tell after I'm gone. I picture my daughters—strong, kind, discerning. I picture my wife's steady faith, my brothers' laughter, the friends who stood beside me when the road turned narrow. I picture the quiet mornings when prayer feels less like talking and more like remembering that you're not alone.

Legacy isn't about being remembered. It's about leaving others better than you found them. It's about grace outliving you.

And reflection? Maybe it's just the light of gratitude shining backward across all the miles you didn't realize you were being carried.

Author's Reflection – The Dance Beyond Collisions

There are moments when the rhythm feels off—when grace and grit seem to play in different keys. But over time, I've come to believe that what sounds like dissonance is often just harmony we don't yet understand.

My father's strength and my mother's gentleness, the courtroom's weight and the whisper of prayer—all of them were movements in the same unfinished song.

I used to think faith was learned in sanctuaries; now I know it's composed in the noise of ordinary days.

I still think about that "world without collisions," the one I first met in *Master Harold … and the Boys*—a place where people move without wounding each other. Maybe heaven will sound like that: perfect rhythm, perfect grace.

Until then, we live in the half-finished music of this life, trusting the Composer who holds the final measure. The One who once turned the world's dissonance into harmony did so on a hill between two thieves. And when the broken one beside Him asked for mercy, the answer was simple and eternal: "Today, you will be with Me in paradise."

That's the hope I hold to—the grace of the Man on the middle cross. The melody of mercy began there, and it's still playing now: in the quiet forgiveness we extend, in the courage to love what's imperfect, and in the grace that finds us even when the music stops.

And maybe that's where the next story begins—*Between Two Thieves*, where Grace Himself hung in the middle, and heaven flung its gates open wide.

ABOUT THE AUTHOR

Gregg A. Stewart is a lifelong Ohioan whose writing reflects an honest walk of faith—one marked by doubt, grace, and the quiet pursuit of truth. He doesn't claim to have all the answers; he simply invites others to walk with him, to *come and see*, as Philip said to Nathanael.

His memoir, *Unreasonable Doubt: When the Call of Duty Becomes a Test of Faith*, was born out of a season of moral and spiritual testing. This companion, *Conversations in Faith and Conscience*, continues that journey—not to resolve every question, but to listen for God in the spaces between them, trusting that mercy is already on the way.

UNREASONABLE DOUBT

A Companion Reflection Series

Conversations in Faith and Conscience —
A Reader's Guide

For those who have walked through doubt
and found grace waiting there

AUTHOR'S NOTE

When I finished writing *Unreasonable Doubt*, I thought I was closing a door. I had said what needed to be said, walked through the shadows, and found my peace in the story God had allowed me to live. But what I didn't expect was how the silence afterward began to speak.

These pages are born from that silence.

They're not a retelling of the book, but a series of conversations that lingered long after the verdict—quiet reflections between faith and doubt, justice and mercy, obedience and surrender. They grew out of my own wrestling, those nights when Scripture felt more like a mirror than a map, and prayer sounded like breathing in the dark.

I began to imagine what it might sound like if faith and reason sat down together and simply talked—two voices, not arguing, but listening. That's what this companion became: a dialogue between the head that seeks understanding and the heart that clings to grace.

Each reflection began as a small ember—a moment in the memoir that refused to go out. Some were born in the courtroom, others in the memories of childhood, others still in the long quiet of hindsight. Together, they trace a simple truth: that God's grace isn't fragile. It holds steady, even when everything else shakes.

If *Unreasonable Doubt* was the story of faith under fire, this companion is faith at rest—faith that still trembles, but no longer fears the trembling.

My prayer is that as you read or listen to these conversations, you'll find echoes of your own. Because doubt doesn't disqualify us from faith; it draws us deeper into it. And sometimes, the most honest prayer we can offer is the one that begins with a whisper:

"Lord, I believe; help Thou my unbelief."

— **Gregg A. Stewart**
Dublin, Ohio

Episode 1 — The Weight of the Gavel

Theme: Faith and conscience under civic duty
Scripture: *"Be still, and know that I am God." — Psalm 46:10 (ESV)*

There's a moment in every calling when duty stops being theoretical. For me, it was the day I walked into a courtroom, expecting routine jury duty and finding instead a test of faith.

The air was solemn, and the marble floors echoed beneath the weight of justice. As Juror Number Eight, I felt the fragile line between law and conscience tighten around me. Across the room sat a man whose future rested in our hands. That realization reshaped every heartbeat.

In that silence, I prayed a prayer I'd said a thousand times before, but never with such gravity: "Lord, let me see the truth—and give me the courage to follow it."

I learned that faith and justice don't always share a common language. But in the courtroom that week, I began to see that justice, when it's pure, is one of God's dialects. It asks us not to play God, but to listen for Him—in the testimony, in the silence, even in our own trembling hesitation.

The gavel fell like a benediction and a warning. Justice demands clarity; faith demands surrender. Somewhere between the two, I began to understand that obedience often looks less like certainty and more like stillness.

Reflection: *Where is God asking you to carry truth with humility today? Are there places where obedience means being still instead of being certain?*

Episode 2 — The Child of Light in Darkness

Theme: Trusting God when the light feels withheld

Scripture: *"Let him who walks in darkness and has no light trust in the name of the Lord and rely on his God." — Isaiah 50:10 (ESV)*

Isaiah speaks of a child of the light walking in darkness—a verse that once puzzled me. What business does light have in the dark?

It took me years to see the answer. God sometimes withholds the light not to abandon us, but to strengthen us. Because faith that only walks by sight never learns to trust.

When the trial ended, I thought I was finished with questions. But the silence that followed was its own kind of darkness—the kind where faith must remember what light once looked like. It was like walking through a familiar house at night: I couldn't see the furniture, but I knew it was there.

In that space, prayer became less about answers and more about presence. Even in the dark, God's voice doesn't vanish; it only softens, becoming an echo that invites trust.

Faith, I've learned, isn't the torch that drives out the dark—it's the hand that keeps reaching for God when you can't see a thing.

Reflection: *What kind of darkness is God using to deepen your trust? Can you still reach for His hand when the light feels gone?*

Episode 3 — A World Without Collisions

Theme: The longing for harmony amid human imperfection
Reference: *Inspired by Athol Fugard's Master Harold … and the Boys*

In Fugard's play, two men imagine a world where people dance without bumping into each other—a world without collisions. The image stayed with me because life rarely moves that smoothly.

My childhood home was filled with collisions: my father's grit, my mother's grace—two worlds under one roof, teaching me that love sometimes comes with bruises and beauty intertwined. We don't escape collisions; we learn to move with them.

I've come to see that faith isn't the absence of collisions—it's the willingness to keep dancing anyway. Even in the courtroom, justice and mercy seemed to pull in different directions, and yet grace somehow moved between them, finding rhythm in the tension.

Maybe that's what heaven will be—a world where love no longer collides with pain, where grace and truth finally move in perfect time. But until then, we keep learning the steps, trusting the Composer who wrote the music.

Reflection: *Where are you learning to dance through imperfection? Can you find grace in the rhythm of what's still unfinished?*

Episode 4 — Faith and Doubt

Theme: The holy tension that refines belief
Scripture: *"Lord, I believe; help Thou my unbelief."* — *Mark 9:24 (KJV)*

For much of my life, I thought doubt disqualified faith. I imagined faith as a clean, unshaken conviction—the kind that never faltered, never questioned, never trembled.

But when I walked through my own valleys of uncertainty, I discovered something I hadn't expected: Doubt isn't the enemy of faith. It's the forge where faith is refined.

Thomas needed to see the wounds. Job needed to ask the questions. Neither was condemned for it. God met them both in their honesty.

Faith, I've learned, isn't the absence of questions—it's the decision to keep the conversation going. It's the prayer that still whispers in the dark: "I don't understand You, Lord, but I'm not leaving."

Unreasonable doubt—the kind that dares to hope even when reason runs out—that's the soil where real belief grows. And maybe the miracle isn't that doubt disappears, but that grace stays long enough to turn it into trust.

Reflection: *What questions have you been afraid to bring to God? Could it be that your honesty is the very place He's waiting to meet you?*

Episode 5 — Fear and Trembling

Theme: Obedience, reverence, and the quiet weight of conscience
Scripture: *"Work out your own salvation with fear and trembling, for it is God who works in you, both to will and to work for His good pleasure." — Philippians 2:12–13 (ESV)*

There's a trembling that doesn't come from fear, but from reverence. It's what happens when you realize you've been trusted with something sacred.

The courtroom taught me that. Judgment isn't only about the accused—it's also about the heart of the one who must decide. To sit in that space was to feel the gravity of obedience.

I used to think "fear and trembling" meant anxiety. Now I believe it means awe—a holy awareness that God's will is unfolding through fragile hands like ours. Even our best intentions rest in His mercy.

Faith doesn't erase that trembling—it sanctifies it. It turns human uncertainty into spiritual reverence. And in that trembling, I found peace—not because I was certain, but because I knew I wasn't alone in the work.

Reflection: *When was the last time you trembled before something holy? What would it look like to see your uncertainty as reverence, not weakness?*

Episode 6 — The Verdict and the Cross

Theme: When judgment meets mercy and the gospel speaks in seven words

Scripture: *"Truly I tell you, today you will be with Me in paradise." — Luke 23:43 (NIV)*

When the verdict was read, the air itself seemed to hold its breath. Justice had spoken, but mercy was still whispering.

That's when the cross came into focus again—not as a symbol, but as a sentence already served. At Calvary, the Lawgiver became the condemned. The Judge took the place of the guilty, so mercy could take the place of despair.

It was there that I learned my seven-word gospel: *The man on the middle cross said I could come.* Seven words that hold the whole of redemption. No theology exam, no merit required—just a thief's last plea and a Savior's last invitation.

The gavel falls, but grace keeps speaking. And when human justice reaches its limit, divine mercy begins its song. That's the true verdict of the cross: Love has already served the sentence.

Reflection: *Do you believe those seven words were meant for you? "The man on the middle cross said I could come." Say them slowly until they find their way into your heart.*

Episode 7 — Legacy and Reflection

Theme: The unfinished music of grace
Scripture: *"When all has been heard, the conclusion of the matter is this: fear God and keep His commandments, for this is the whole duty of man." — Ecclesiastes 12:13 (CSB)*

Legacy isn't about what we leave behind—it's about how we live while we're still here. It's written in the small, unseen moments: in the way we forgive, the way we speak truth with love, the way grace outlasts anger.

My father taught me grit. My mother taught me grace. Together, they gave me the rhythm I still move by. I used to think those two notes clashed. Now I hear them as harmony—the rough and the tender playing in time.

Life, faith, justice—they're all imperfect dances. But we keep moving, trusting the Composer who knows how to turn dissonance into beauty. And when the music finally resolves, it will sound like mercy.

Reflection: *What song is your life teaching those who will come after you? Can you hear both grit and grace in its melody?*

Closing Benediction —
Grace Outliving the Verdict

There are moments when faith feels like standing in a courtroom, waiting for a verdict that may never come. But the longer I walk with God, the more I realize the verdict has already been spoken: *Forgiven.*

Grace outlives every accusation. It survives every doubt, every trembling prayer, every season where light seems gone. Because grace is not a moment—it's a Person. And the Man on the middle cross still says, "You can come."

So I will.

And I'll keep walking, keep believing, and keep listening for the rhythm of mercy until the world without collisions becomes home.

UNREASONABLE DOUBT

Leader's Guide

Conversations in Faith & Conscience —
A Facilitator's Manual

For Pastors • Small-Group Leaders • Men's Ministries
Recovery Ministries • Discipleship Circles

INTRODUCTION FOR LEADERS

This guide is designed to help you lead honest, grace-filled conversations using the *Unreasonable Doubt* Companion Reflection Series. Unlike typical study guides, these sessions are built around **story, reflection, and conscience**, not academic lecture. Your role is not to answer every question—but to **create a safe place for truth to surface**.

Leader Principles

1. **Honor the room**—create safety, confidentiality, and respect.
2. **Honor the story**—Gregg's journey is one man's testimony, not theology.
3. **Honor the Spirit**—leave room for silence, tears, conviction, and grace.
4. **Honor pacing**—conversations cannot be forced. Truth unfolds.

Recommended Format

1. **7 sessions** (one per episode)
2. **60–75 minutes each**

Suitable for men's groups, mixed groups, or one-on-one discipleship.

SESSION 1 — *Episode 1: The Weight of the Gavel*

Theme: Faith and conscience under civic duty

Scripture: *Psalm 46:10* — "Be still, and know that I am God."

Session Goals

- Explore how God meets us in responsibility and moral tension.
- Reflect on obedience when clarity is not available.
- Identify places in life where conscience is under strain.

Leader Opening (Read Aloud)

"Today we begin by entering the space where faith and duty collide. Jury duty became a crucible where Gregg learned that justice demands clarity, and faith demands surrender. Let's explore what that tension looks like in our lives."

Discussion Questions

1. When have you been placed in a role where someone else's life or outcome depended on your judgment?
2. What does *being still* look like for you in moments of pressure?
3. Is there an area of your life right now where obedience feels uncertain?
4. How do you discern between fear, emotion, and the quiet voice of God?

Leader Insight

People often think "faith under pressure" means being bold. Actually, it often looks like **humility, hesitation, and listening**.

Prayer Focus

Ask God for clarity, courage, and the stillness needed to hear Him under pressure.

SESSION 2 — *Episode 2: The Child of Light in Darkness*

Theme: Trusting God when the light feels withheld
Scripture: *Isaiah 50:10*

Session Goals

- Explore how God uses seasons of obscurity.
- Normalize spiritual darkness as part of Christian maturity.
- Learn to trust in God's character when His presence feels distant.

Discussion Questions

1. When have you walked through a season where God felt silent?
2. What emotions surface when light is withheld—anger, fear, numbness?
3. What anchors your faith when you cannot sense God at all?
4. How might God be strengthening trust in your current season?

Leader Insight

Darkness is not abandonment—it is often preparation.

Prayer Focus

Invite God to meet participants in their hidden places and deepen trust.

SESSION 3 — *Episode 3: A World Without Collisions*

Theme: Grace within imperfection and emotional complexity
Reference: *Master Harold … and the Boys*

Session Goals

- Explore how faith persists in messy families and broken stories.
- Recognize the collisions in our own relationships.
- Learn to see grace as movement, not perfection.

Discussion Questions

1. What collisions shaped your early understanding of love or faith?
2. In what relationships are you still learning to "dance through imperfection"?
3. How do grit and grace show up in your story?
4. Where might God be composing harmony in a place that feels dissonant?

Leader Insight

This session often opens deep wounds—move gently. Honor vulnerability.

Prayer Focus

Ask for healing in relationships where collisions have left bruises.

SESSION 4 — *Episode 4: Faith and Doubt*

Theme: Doubt as refinement

Scripture: *Mark 9:24* — "Help Thou my unbelief."

Session Goals

- Free participants from shame around doubt.
- Demonstrate that doubt and faith coexist.
- Invite honest wrestling as part of discipleship.

Discussion Questions

1. What kinds of doubt have you felt but never voiced?
2. Who taught you that doubt was dangerous or shameful?
3. How might bringing your doubt to God deepen your trust?
4. What does "unreasonable doubt" mean in your own spiritual life?

Leader Insight

This is often the most transformative session—because people finally say out loud, "I don't understand God right now."

Prayer Focus

A prayer of honesty: "Lord, meet us in our unanswered questions."

SESSION 5 — *Episode 5: Fear and Trembling*

Theme: Reverence, obedience, and the weight of conscience
Scripture: *Philippians 2:12–13*

Session Goals

- Understand reverence as obedience with humility.
- Examine areas where God is calling for courageous integrity.
- See trembling as worship, not weakness.

Discussion Questions

1. When have you felt the "weight" of obedience?
2. How do you discern God's will when choices feel morally complex?
3. What scares you more—being wrong, or being responsible?
4. How has God worked through your trembling, not your confidence?

Leader Insight

Many men especially have never framed trembling as a **holy** posture. Let them.

Prayer Focus

Pray for courage to obey without full clarity.

SESSION 6 — *Episode 6: The Verdict and the Cross*

Theme: Judgment, mercy, and the seven-word gospel

Scripture: "Today you will be with Me in paradise." — Luke 23:43

Session Goals

- See the cross as the ultimate verdict of mercy.
- Understand that grace is not earned—it is spoken.
- Connect human justice with divine redemption.

Discussion Questions

1. How do you relate to the thief on the cross?
2. What do the seven words—*"The man on the middle cross said I could come"*—stir in you?
3. Where do you still fear judgment or disqualification?
4. How has God shown mercy in places where you expected punishment?

Leader Insight

This session often brings tears—allow silence and reverence.

Prayer Focus

A prayer of receiving grace.

SESSION 7 — *Episode 7: Legacy and Reflection*

Theme: The unfinished music of grace

Scripture: *Ecclesiastes 12:13*

Session Goals

- Understand legacy as daily faithfulness, not accomplishment.
- Integrate family stories into spiritual identity.
- Reflect on how grit and grace form a lifelong testimony.

Discussion Questions

1. What legacy was handed to you—both good and painful?
2. What legacy do you want to hand to your children or community?
3. Where is God rewriting your story through grace?
4. What "unfinished music" do you sense God still composing in you?

Leader Insight

This final session is the moment to celebrate growth and healing.

Prayer Focus

Dedicate each life to the ongoing work of grace.

Closing Blessing for the Leader to Read

"Grace outlives every verdict spoken over your life. Every doubt, every fear, every trembling moment is held in the hands of the Man on the middle cross. Walk in His mercy. Rest in His love. And let your life sing the unfinished music of grace."

www.ingramcontent.com/pod-product-compliance
Lightning Source LLC
LaVergne TN
LVHW090328210926
848480LV00004B/1337
* 9 7 9 8 9 0 1 8 3 0 3 6 9 *